WHO'S WHOOO AMONG THE OWLS?

NATALIE TOTIRE

NTCreations
www.natalietcreations.com
e-mail: ntcreations@live.com

This Book Belongs To

_____

Given By

_____

When the sun goes down,
the moon comes out at night.

The owls begin to fly
in the soft moonlight.

There are many different
kinds of owls,
flying silently and free:

Owls that live in deserts,
and owls that live in trees.

The Great Horned Owl is very big.
He says "Hoo Hoo Hoo Hoo!"

The horns on his head are not ears,
but feather tufts of two.

The Screech Owl is smaller.
They can be red or gray.

They do not hoot, but whinny like
a horse. "N-n-e-e-e-i-i-i-g-g-h!"

The Barred Owl has no
feather tufts at all.

And when he calls, it sounds like:
"Who Cooks for You? Who Cooks
for You All?"

The Snowy Owl lives in the arctic,
where it is very cold.

But they like to wander very far,
to places untold.

The Elf Owl lives in the desert,
where it is hot and dry.

Yet they never make a sound
when they lift their wings to fly.

The Burrowing Owls possess
a very special skill.

They like to live in tunnels,
then roost upon a hill.

Barn Owls got their name
from nesting in the barns.

They would catch the mice
for farmers,
and keep their crops from harm.

The Short-eared Owl has
tiny tufts of feathers on its head.

It roosts near the green pastures
or places it feels led.

The Spotted Owl lives among
the giant Redwood Trees.

It loves the deep, dark woods,
and nests where no man sees.

The Eagle Owl,
at two feet tall,
of all the owls, is tallest.

The little Elf Owl,
six inches tall,
of all the owls, is smallest.

Isn't it amazing?
Did you know...

the Great Gray Owl has
wonderful hearing and
large eyes that bestow?

The owls have such soft feathers.
Colors help them hide in trees,
with patterns that blend easy
in ways so no man sees!

Whooo knows the
wonders of the owl's
design?

When night is done,
owls hide and sleep.
To find the owl,
look very deep.

Look at the wonderful world.
Can YOU find the owl?

About the Author

Natalie Totire is an author, illustrator, and child care worker who loves to paint, using watercolors and acrylics. Her paintings have won numerous awards at the DuPage Art League of Wheaton, Illinois, where she has been a member since 2004. She is also a member of Phi Theta Kappa and of the Society of Children's Book Writers and Illustrators (SCBWI).

Using layers of acrylic paint, these illustrations were either based on sketches of live owls from Willowbrook Wildlife Center (Glen Ellyn, IL) or from taxiderms. The Short-eared Owl and the Screech Owls were mostly painted from life.

Her web site is: www.natalietcreations.com
E-mail address is: ntcreations@live.com

www.ingramcontent.com/pod-product-compliance
Lightning Source LLC
Chambersburg PA
CBHW041533280526
45792CB00004B/1482